Marvels of Creation

Breathtaking Birds

BUDDY & KAY DAVI

Marvels of Creation
Breathtaking Birds

First Printing, January 2006
Second Printing, July 2012

Master Books® is a division of the New Leaf Publishing Group, Inc.

Previously published as *Special Wonders of Our Feathered Friends*.

ISBN: 978-0-89051-457-3
Library of Congress Number: 2005933268

Please visit our website for other great titles:
www.masterbooks.net

For information regarding author interviews, please contact the publicity department at (870) 438-5288.

Printed in China

Acknowledgments

Writing a book is a team effort, and we have the best team anyone could ask for: the Answers in Genesis staff. Special thanks go to Brandon Vallorani and Dan Zordel for their hard work and dedication to this project.

— Buddy & Kay Davis

Illustrations by Buddy Davis

We would like to thank Stephen Kirkpatrick, Peter Weber, and Mike Williams with the Ohio Dept. of Natural Resources for use of their photos.

Contents

Introduction

One of God's most magnificent creations is the bird. How many of us have awakened on a spring morning with the cheerful song of a wren or have fallen asleep as a whippoorwill chanting a lonely lullaby makes unforgettable memories? Their vibrant array of colors — some iridescent and even the earth tones — and striking patterns of feathers show the creativeness of the Master's hand, which fashioned them.

Because of their ability to fly, birds have long intrigued man, causing them to be studied more than any other class of animal. The Word of God teaches that birds were created on the fifth day of creation: "And God said, Let the waters bring forth abundantly the moving creature that hath life and fowl that may fly above the earth in the open firmament of heaven. And God created great whales, and every living creature that moveth, which the waters brought forth abundantly, after their kind, and every winged fowl after his kind: and God saw that it was good. And God blessed them saying, Be fruitful and multiply, and fill the waters in the seas, and let the fowl multiply in the earth. And the evening and the morning were the fifth day" (Gen. 1:20–23).

It is sad that in our time of earth history, some scoff at the clear teaching of God and praise the godless theory of evolution, using the false theory of millions of years to explain away the creation and the Creator. Evolution replaces God with time, matter, and chance, coupled with mutations that somehow make pond scum fly.

"For the invisible things of him from the creation of the world are clearly seen, being understood by the things that are made, even his eternal power and Godhead; so that they are without excuse; Because that, when they knew God, they glorified him not as God, neither were thankful; but became vain in their imaginations and their foolish heart was darkened. Professing themselves to be wise, they became fools" (Rom. 1:22).

Most paleontologists and ornithologists are bent on advocating the evolution from reptile to bird. Some promote this impossibility as fact by pointing to certain homologies found in therapod dinosaur skeletons showing this evolutionary link. We read about this in major magazines, books, newspapers, TV, well-funded film documentaries, and motion pictures with unlimited budgets. The evolutionists have cleverly used the illusion of evolution along with millions of years to interpret the fossil record. They speak and write about their findings with unchallenged authority backed by a godless media. The world is duped into believing a lie. The dinosaur-to-bird link is postulated so much that leading authorities in the field of paleontology have stated that the next time you see a flock of geese flying overhead, you can say the dinosaurs are migrating. Some have gone so far as to state that when you eat a chicken dinner, you can say you are eating dinosaurs.

Evolutionists often use evidence of microevolution (changes within a kind) to prove their theories. It is true; we do see changes within a kind, however, the Bible states in Genesis that God created the different kinds, and from them, we know that different species have developed through the centuries. Those believing in creation certainly accept this. Citing these developments as evidence, evolutionists believe macroevolution (changes from one kind to another) has definitely happened. This is where creationists and evolutionists differ sharply in the interpretations of the evidence.

The fossil record is an embarrassment to the evolutionists because of the absence of the necessary intermediate forms. One kind evolving into another has never been found although many evolutionists claim they have found hundreds or thousands of examples. When hard pressed to come up with one unrefuted example, they cannot do so. Some try to use Archaeopteryx, an ancient bird which even most evolutionists today admit was a fully functioning bird. Some claim the different varieties of finches on the Galapagos Islands are proof of evolution. However, the finches are still finches and have not changed into any other kind of bird. No macroevolution is at work there; it is a good example of microevolution.

Paleontologists working with skilled artists try to influence public opinion by painting dinosaurs with feathers. Some of them go so far as to believe and teach that baby dinosaur hatchlings such as *T. rex* may have been covered with down. Meanwhile, instead of rebuking such anti-biblical teaching, most church leaders simply ignore this brainwashing and preach the same non-offensive sermons over and over again. They do not want to "ruffle the feathers" of any evolutionary scholars in the congregation; God help us. Romans 10:14 reminds us, " . . and how shall they hear without a preacher?"

It's about time that we as Christians point fingers at science, falsely so called, and arm the congregation with the full armor of God (Eph. 6:11). This will help us defend our faith. "But sanctify the Lord God in your hearts: and be ready always to give an answer to every man that asketh you a reason of the hope that is in you with meekness and fear:" (1 Pet. 3:15.) The world is seeking answers and we need to provide them.

Regrettably, we are not even jolted when pastors and church leaders are indoctrinated into evolutionary concepts themselves. Trying to reconcile the Bible with millions of years of evolution, they ignore the fact that there could have been no death before sin. Compromising God's clear teachings, they are more concerned about offending the people than offending the Lord. And we ask what is wrong.

The necessary process of changing a reptile into a bird would be an absurdity requiring innumerable favorable mutations. First, it necessitates that a cold-blooded specimen be changed into a warm-blooded one. Next, the size of the brain would have to increase — birds have a much larger brain than reptiles. Birds have totally different blood and respiratory systems than reptiles. Reptiles hiss while birds sing. Not to mention the fact that it is impossible for a scale to change into the intricate design of a feather. No scale which has partially evolved into a feather has ever been found. The first time we find a feather in the fossil record, it is fully formed.

Evolutionists often ignore or purposely fail to show the public the true facts, and at the same time they put down creation as a non-scientific and pseudo-science. The Bible warns of this in 2 Peter 3:3–6: "Knowing this first, that there shall come in the last days scoffers, walking after their own lusts, And saying, Where is the promise of his coming? For since the fathers fell asleep, all things continue as they were from the beginning of the creation. For this they willingly are ignorant of, that by the word of God, the heavens were of old, and the earth standing out of the water and in the water: Whereby the world that then was, being overflowed with water, perished." First Timothy 6:20: "O Timothy, keep that which is committed to thy trust, avoiding profane and vain babblings, and oppositions of science falsely so called."

Just for the record, there are now thousands of qualified scientists from all fields around the world who have turned their back on evolution because of the lack of evidence, and they are convinced of the record of earth's history as presented in the Bible.

This book is different from most nature books in that it seeks to honor God as Creator and give all glory to Him. As humans created in the image of God, we should notice and appreciate His work. Even the world in its cursed state (because of the fall of Adam) can still show beauty, design, and purpose. From the tiny intricate tail of the hummingbird to the beautiful fan of a peacock's tail, the artistry of the Creator is shown. We hope you enjoy this work and that you will be amazed at the marvelous design of birds and their God-given ability to survive in their environment. "For by him were all things created" (Col. 1:16).

When God created birds on the fifth day, everything was good. Birds were plant eaters in the beginning along with all of God's creation (Gen. 1:29–30). After sin (brought about by the disobedience of Adam and Eve) entered our world, things changed. It was at this time that behavior changes occurred and some birds became carnivorous. We have the pre-conceived idea that claws, talons, fangs, and sharp-pointed beaks indicate that a creature is and always has been a meat eater. Hawks, owls, and eagles have beaks used to kill and rip prey apart. However, a parrot has a beak very similar to these raptors, but it only eats seeds.

We need to look at nature in light of God's Word. It is only then that the things we see in today's world will make sense and have purpose.

Just as God cares for the birds, so much more He cares for you. Sin is what separates man from the Holy God, but God's Son, Jesus Christ paid the price for our sin when He died on the cross in our place. We simply must believe in faith that Christ has atoned for our sins. If you haven't yet put faith in Him for salvation, please do so. Read John 3:16 and Romans 10:9–10.

Luke 12:6–7: "Are not five sparrows sold for two farthings, and not one of them is forgotten before God? But even the very hairs of your head are all numbered. Fear not therefore: ye are of more value than many sparrows."

Arctic Tern

The arctic tern inhabits the coastal waters, lakes, and marshlands of the northern parts of Europe, Asia, and North America. It is a medium-gray color with a black cap and nape. It is pale underneath and has a bright red bill. The arctic tern has short legs and a long, forked tail.

What is truly amazing about the arctic tern is its migratory route. Every year it travels up to 24,000 miles (38,400 km) to winter at the Antarctic Ocean and then return to its nesting grounds.

This bird nests in colonies between May and July near the water on a sandy patch of ground. They often pick deserted islands for their nesting sites. The female lays two eggs, which are incubated by both parents for about 20 to 22 days. The hatchlings can swim within two days and can fly in about 20 days. Both parents continue feeding them even after they have left the nest.

At the end of the summer, the young tern knows what direction, how far, and at what time he needs to start the migratory trip. God has placed in the arctic tern a very wonderful guidance system that leaves man marveling.

The arctic tern feeds mainly on fish. It flies low over the water with its head down looking for prey. When it locates a fish, it plucks it out of the water or half-dives after it. It can swim, but not for long periods at a time. It also eats mollusks and insects.

Arctic Tern

CHARADRIIFORMES • LARIDAE • STERNA PARADISAEA

WEIGHT: 4-1/4 ounces (119 grams)

LENGTH: 14-1/2inches (36 cm)

LIFE SPAN: Oldest known 3-4 years

SPECIAL DESIGN FEATURE: The arctic tern was created with exceptional migratory instincts taking it on a journey from the Arctic to the Antarctic and back every year.

DID YOU KNOW? The migratory route of the arctic tern is approximately 24,000 miles (38,400 km) round trip every year and it probably sees more daylight in its lifetime than any other animal.

Atlantic Puffin

The puffin, also known as the sea parrot, is a popular and easily recognized sea bird. This species makes its home in the North Atlantic and Arctic Oceans. It rarely comes to shore except when it is time to lay its eggs.

The puffin has a very colorful large beak during the breeding season. The bill has red, yellow, and blue stripes with yellow skin in the corner of the mouth. After the breeding season, the colors are shed leaving the bill smaller and gray in color. The feathers of the puffin are black on the upper part of the body and white underneath with the black continuing under the neck like a collar. The puffin has a small colored patch above and below its eyes as well. The puffin has an oil gland located near its tail. It applies this oil to its feathers to keep them waterproof.

Its wings enable the puffin to swim at great depths hunting for food. The inside of the beak has backward-pointing spikes to help hold its food. The favorite food of the puffin is the sand eel, but it also catches small fish, mollusks, and other plankton animals.

Puffins usually pair for life although they don't stay together all of the time. They congregate in large colonies during the breeding season, which lasts from March through April. When it's time to build a nest, both the male and female go on shore and start digging burrows or cleaning out old ones. They even use abandoned rabbit burrows. A single egg is laid at the end of a six-foot long (1.8 m) tunnel and is incubated by both parents. The egg will hatch in 40 to 43 days. Both parents will feed the new hatchling until it is six weeks old. The chick will then leave the burrow and find its way to the sea at night to lessen the danger of being eaten by predators. Although it cannot fly at this time, it is a good swimmer and will dive if a threat of danger appears. The young chick will return to the colony the following year but will not breed until it is 4 to 5 years old.

The predators of the puffin include all the large sea birds such as gulls. At one time, man hunted the puffin for food and used its feathers for decoration.

Atlantic Puffin

CHARADRIIFORMES • ALCIDAE
FRATERCULA ARCTICA

WEIGHT: 12–17 ounces (490.5 gr)

LENGTH: 12 inches (30 cm)

SPECIAL DESIGN FEATURE: The puffin has backward pointing spikes inside the beak to help hold its food.

DID YOU KNOW? Puffins live in the cold arctic waters and they rarely come on land except to lay their eggs.

Bald Eagle

Bald eagles can usually be sighted near rivers, lakes, or the ocean, perched in trees or atop bluffs. When it soars, the eagle can be easily distinguished from a vulture because it holds its wings outstretched in a flat horizontal position — not uplifted in a "V" like the vulture. The white head and neck distinguish the bald eagle from other eagles. The white head is the sign of a mature bird at least four or five years old. A younger bird has brown plumage on its head and can be confused with an immature golden eagle. The mature bald eagle also has a white tail, a brownish-black body, and yellow feet and bill. Both sexes look alike; however, the female may be larger than the male.

The breeding season of the eagle is dependent upon the latitude at which the eagle lives. For instance, in Florida, the season is November through January. In Alaska, the season is March through May.

The nest of the eagle is called an aerie and is made of a pile of sticks in a tree approximately 20 to 30 feet (6.1–9.15 m) above the ground. The nest can be as much as 7 feet (1.1 m) across and 11 feet (1.8 m) deep. These nests are added to and repaired each season. Coastal eagles may build their nests on the ground, lined with soft grass, sticks, feathers, and moss. Inside the nest, the eagle will lay one to three unmarked white eggs. Both parents share incubation and in approximately 35 days the young are hatched. Usually only one survives to leave the nest in 10 to 11 weeks.

With both monocular and binocular vision, an eagle has keen eyes for spotting prey. It moves its eyes very little and can see by rotating its head nearly a full circle like an owl. Ornithologists report that an eagle can spot prey up to two miles away.

Eagles are excellent fishers and fish are the mainstay of their diet. They also eat small mammals, birds, and carrion. Eagles kill their prey by grasping it with their feet and spiking their sharp talons into the victim. They can tear the meat with their sharp bill. Bald eagles often steal food from the osprey. They can dive at 200 mph and they fly approximately 30 mph.

Eagles sometimes concentrate in large numbers in places of abundant food, such as the ten-mile stretch of the Chilkat River in Alaska where 3,500 or more may gather to feed on dead salmon. Eagles were once numerous, but hunting, pesticides, and habitat destruction cut their numbers down to less than 1,000 pairs by the mid-1970s. Declared an endangered species in 1978, the eagle's survival has become a fantastic success story with over 5,700 pairs counted by the U.S. Fish and Wildlife Service in 1998. They thrive in Alaska and Florida and can be seen in increasing numbers in many other areas.

Bald Eagle

FALCONIFORMES • ACCIPITRIDAE
HALIAEETUS LEUCOCEPHALUS

WEIGHT: 10–14 pounds (4.6 kg–6.3 kg)

LENGTH: 33–42 inches (85–105 cm)

WING SPAN: up to 8 feet (2.45 m)

LIFE SPAN: 25–30 years

SPECIAL DESIGN FEATURE: Eagles possess both monocular and binocular vision with incredible eyesight.

DID YOU KNOW? On June 20, 1798, the bald eagle was adopted as the national bird of the United States of America.

Black Skimmer

Skimmers are nicknamed scissorbills because of the design of their beak. They live by large rivers, lakes, lagoons, estuaries, marshes, and the seacoast but do not venture out far to sea. The black skimmer prefers the inland waters of the tropical Pacific and Atlantic coasts of North America. It is the largest of the three skimmers. The other two are the African and Indian skimmer.

The wings of the black skimmer are long, narrow, and pointed and it has a forked tail. The webbed feet are at the end of short, reddish legs. The body is brownish-black above and white underneath. Males and females look alike, but females are smaller than males. A unique feature among these birds is the vertical cat-like pupil in the eye. The beak is black in front and red behind. Black skimmers sound something like a pack of hounds baying at a treed animal.

Most hunting is done in the evening. The special design of the skimmer allows it to hunt for food in a unique way. The lower mandible is longer than the upper, allowing the bird to fly inches above the water, "skimming" the surface, with the lower mandible cutting into the water. In this manner, it feeds on fish and other small aquatic creatures. Strong neck muscles help snap the prey out of the water. The bill has sharp edges near the base which keep the slippery fish from sliding out of the mouth.

Skimmers are sociable, nesting, feeding, and roosting in flocks. These birds nest in loose colonies with the nest consisting of a hollow depression in the sand. They will usually lay four or five buff black-spotted eggs, which are incubated by the female. Both parents feed the young hatchlings, but it's not long before the chicks leave the nest. Hatchlings are camouflaged and nearly invisible as they crouch in the sand. The bills of the young are equal in length when they hatch so they can feed on the ground, picking up small pieces of food. As the feathers begin to grow, so does the lower half of the bill. At approximately six weeks of age, the young skimmers start to fly.

Black Skimmer

CHARADRIFORMES • RYNCHOPIDAE RYNCHOPS NIGRA

LENGTH: 18 inches (45 cm)

LIFE SPAN: 12–15 years

SPECIAL DESIGN FEATURE: God designed the lower bill of the skimmer to grow longer than the upper. This allows the skimmer to fly close to the water and funnel water around the beak so it can catch aquatic life.

DID YOU KNOW? Skimmers can stay airborne close to the water without allowing their wings to drag in the water.

Brown Pelican

Pelicans are the largest of all the aquatic birds and are famous for the large pouch of skin hanging from their lower jaw. Eight species of pelican can be found in North America on the West Coast and in the marshlands of the southeast. The brown pelican lives along the coastline of California and Mexico inhabiting the rocks and cliffs near the warm coastal waters. They seldom fly far inland and do not go far from the shore out to sea.

The brown pelican is a large bird with brown-gray feathers overall and a wide white band on either side of its neck. The long beak is pale yellow with a pouch of bare skin beneath the lower jaw.

Sometimes brown pelicans gather in flocks of up to 50 birds to roost and feed together. They feed almost entirely on fish, which they catch by diving from heights of up to 65 feet (19.8 m). They plunge into the sea scooping up a beak full of water and fish. With the water in its pouch, it is too heavy to fly so it sits on the water's surface, waiting for the water to drain away before it can swallow the fish. The sound of the splash as the pelican hits the water can be heard up to half a mile away. A series of air pockets in its chest help to cushion the force of impact and protect it from injury. The air pockets in the chest are part of the bird's lungs.

Pelicans that live in freshwater lakes work in groups forcing fish into a school by beating their wings on the water. Then, using their beaks, they scoop the fish into their pouches.

The brown pelican mates in the spring, building its nest in shallow depressions on the ground, lining it with feathers, and surrounding it with a wall of soil. Some nest in trees, building their home with reeds on a stick platform.

Both adults share in incubating three eggs for approximately four weeks. The chicks are naked when they hatch but have a coat of down within two weeks. The parents feed their young with regurgitated fish.

The brown pelican has few enemies, but it is greatly affected by pesticides. The young are very vulnerable to predators, and occasionally an adult may be killed by sea lions or sharks.

Brown Pelican

PELECANIFORMES • PELECANIDAE
PELECANUS OCCIDENTALIS

LENGTH: 42–54 inches (105–135 cm)
WEIGHT: 15–31 pounds (7–14 kg)
LIFE SPAN: 15–25 years
SPECIAL DESIGN FEATURE: Pelicans use their pouch to catch fish, not to carry them. They can scoop up more than two gallons (8 liters) of water in their pouch.
DID YOU KNOW? The brown pelican can dive from heights of up to 65 feet (19.8 m).

Canada Goose

Seeing the famous "V" formation of the Canada goose is always a blessing to anyone who loves and appreciates nature. Contrary to popular belief, it is not usually the wise old gander that leads the flock but his mate. Leadership of the "V" formation changes from time to time as the lead bird tires. This unique flight pattern restricts drag because of turbulence created by the goose flying ahead. They are capable of obtaining flying speeds of 50–60 miles (80–96 km) per hour and sometimes fly one mile (1.6 km) high. When they take off from the water, they usually run for several steps on the surface flapping their powerful wings to become airborne. Canada geese are also called "honkers" because of their loud vocal call.

The Canada goose is easily recognized by its black head, long neck, and white chin marking that protrudes in back of the eyes. The upper body is a gray-brown while the breast and belly are pale to dark. The tail is black with white underparts. It has a dark gray beak and the legs and webbed feet are the same color.

Canada geese are intelligent and soon learn how to stay clear of danger. However, they can be decoyed and called in by waiting hunters. The meat is delicious and served on many a table during the goose season.

The Canada goose can be found abundantly in Canada and the United States and its range is extending. Pairs mate for life but if one dies, the other mate usually seeks out a partner the following season.

The nest is usually made on the ground near water but they will build on muskrat huts, beaver dams, rocks, and abandoned osprey nests as well. The female lays six to seven eggs and incubates them for 25 to 30 days. Upon hatching, parents immediately lead the goslings to water. Day-old babies can swim up to 40 feet (12.2 m) underwater while feeding or to escape danger.

The young will migrate with their parents in the fall and stay with them in their winter grounds. The family then migrates north in the spring and the yearlings separate at the breeding grounds. Some geese do not migrate.

Canada geese feed mainly in the morning and early evening. They are grazing birds and feed on a variety of grasses and crops. On water, they feed on surface plants but enjoy insects, crustaceans, mollusks, and snails as well.

Canada Goose

ANSERIFORMES • ANATIDAE
BRANTA CANADENSIS

LENGTH: 25–45 inches (64–114 cm)

WEIGHT: 9–14 pounds (4–6 kg)

LIFE SPAN: 20–30 years

SPECIAL DESIGN FEATURE: Canada geese fly in a "V" formation, which reduces drag as the flock flies.

DID YOU KNOW? Canada geese mate for life and the goslings will stay with the parents for a year, even migrating with them.

Cassowary

This very shy bird is from the rain forests of New Guinea and Northern Australia. The cassowary is a large, stocky bird that cannot fly. Short, heavy legs covered with horny plates and broad, very powerful feet support its large body. It has three toes with the inner toe having a very strong and sharp claw which can slice and tear. While these birds are timid, they can be very dangerous if cornered.

The feathers of the cassowary are a glossy black with a blue reflection. Its head is a beautiful blue with a red wattle. The head has a horny growth like a helmet called a casque. It is thought that this helmet is used like a shovel to rake through the leaves to find fallen fruit and possibly to protect its head as it runs through the rainforest. Some indigenous Papuans have observed it using the casque to knock fruit from small trees by ramming the trunks with it.

The cassowary can run up to 31 mph (50 km/h).

The female cassowary is larger than the male. They lead solitary lives except in the breeding season. The female lays 3 to 4 pea-green eggs on the ground which the male will incubate for 55 days. When the eggs hatch, the chicks are striped. Consequently, the male is the parent who will care for the chicks for about nine months.

Their diet consists mainly of fruit. They have been known to swallow fruit such as bananas whole.

The only known enemies of the cassowary are man, dogs, and vehicles.

Cassowary

CASUARIFORMES • CASUARIDAE
CASUARIUS CASUARIUS

HEIGHT: 3-1/4 feet (1 m)
WEIGHT: 190 pounds (85 kg)
LENGTH: 5-1/4 feet (1.6 m)
SPECIAL DESIGN FEATURE: The cassowary has a horny helmet known as a casque that may serve to protect its head as it runs through thick vegetation.
DID YOU KNOW? The nail of the inner toe of the cassowary can grow to be over 4 inches (10 cm) long and is very sharp.

Common Loon

The lonesome call of a loon has been likened to a yodel, laughter, or a cry. Once heard, you will never forget it. The loon's legs are placed far back on its body making walking a chore, but in the water this magnificent bird paddles and dives with style and grace. When searching for small fish to eat, loons can dive 160 feet (49 m) or more and remain underwater for 40 seconds to a minute. (When pursued by an enemy, loons may remain under water for as long as three minutes.) They also eat crustaceans, snails, leeches, mollusks, frogs, insects, crayfish, and salamanders.

The male loon is larger than the female. The head of the loon is black and the body is black with white marks. The neck has a white band and the belly is white. The black beak is long and pointed. Unlike most birds, the bones of the loon are mostly solid, aiding in underwater activities. The loon was created for diving with a streamlined, submersible body. Loons are not ducks. Ducks paddle by moving one foot at a time while loons kick both feet simultaneously, propelling them quickly under water. They steer with their wings.

As for flight, takeoff isn't easy and a loon needs a watery runway. While in the water, it raises itself by beating its wings for propulsion across the surface, taking 20 yards (18.4 m) or more to become airborne. Once airborne, it has an airspeed of 62 mph (99.2 km/hr).

Loons usually sleep on the water but sometimes swim to shore to nap. Nesting on islands or sheltered coves near the water, the loon's nest is made up of grasses, twigs, and rushes. Some may build on muskrat houses. The nests are used year after year and it is believed that loons mate for life. The female lays one to four greenish-brown eggs with dark spots on them around the middle of May. Both parents incubate the eggs, which will hatch in about 29 days, and both raise the chicks.

From day one, the chicks learn to eat whole small fish and plants. The youngsters may ride on the parents' backs but by 10 to 15 days old, they are skilled swimmers and divers. They learn to fly in about 12 weeks.

The range of the loon includes Iceland, Greenland, Canada, and the northern United States. They winter along the Atlantic coast as far south as Florida and along the West Coast from southern Alaska to Baja, California. The Texas coast along the Gulf of Mexico is also a winter haven for the loon.

Common Loon

GAVIIFORMES • GAVIIDAE • GAVIA IMMER

WEIGHT: 9.2 pounds (4.2 kg)

LENGTH: 31 inches (80 cm)

WING SPAN: 51 inches (130 cm)

LIFE SPAN: 7-1/2 years

SPECIAL DESIGN FEATURE: Loons can swim and dive with grace because of placement of their legs and webbed feet.

DID YOU KNOW? Loons need at least 20 yards (18.4 m) for takeoff in order to become airborne.

Common Raven

The raven is the largest member of the crow family and also the largest songbird. It can be found almost anywhere in the Northern Hemisphere including North America, Greenland, northern Africa, Asia, and Europe. Ravens are also found in Nicaragua.

The raven has a heavy, Roman-shaped beak. It is black all over but has a violet and green iridescent sheen when the sun strikes its feathers.

The raven is mentioned 11 times in the Bible. It is the first creature Noah released to try to find land after the global flood (Gen. 8:7). The American Indians of the Northwest believed the raven was a symbol of divinity; contrariwise, the raven was a symbol of evil during medieval times. Aesop used the raven as the main subject of a few fables and Edgar Allan Poe immortalized the raven in his famous poem.

The raven and other crows are believed to be the most intelligent of all birds. They can learn to emulate human words and the sounds of other animals and pets. The raven is cunning, mischievous, and playful, being known to steal (or borrow) trinkets and keep them stored in secret places. Tame birds make entertaining pets. Their call is a deep call of "corronk."

Ravens live in mountainous regions, as well as cliffs, lowland woods, seacoasts, banks of rivers, and treeless tundra, sometimes gathering in large flocks of up to 200. Although ravens are considered by some to be cowards, they can be aggressive when defending their territory. For the most part, they are scavengers and will eat almost anything. They sometimes hunt small mammals, birds, reptiles, and will also gather and store acorns and grains.

Ravens are graceful fliers with powerful, regular wingbeats. They can soar, hover, and do acrobatic somersaults, tumbles, and dives. In flight, the raven can be distinguished from the common crow by its wedge-shaped tail and large size.

Ravens mate for life with most pairs using the same nest year after year. The nest is built by both male and female out of large twigs packed together with mud and lined with grass, wool, hair, moss, etc. Between four and six pale greenish-blue eggs with brown spots are incubated by the hen for three weeks. When the chicks are born, both parents leave the nest and roost in a nearby tree. This habit has given the raven a reputation of being an unkind parent. The Book of Psalms reads, "He giveth to the beast his food and to the young ravens which cry" (Ps.147:9). Both parents feed the chicks and in five to six weeks the young can fly and will leave home.

Common Raven

PASSERIFORMES • CORVIDAE • CORVUS CORAX

WEIGHT: 2.2–3.0 pounds (1–1.33 kg)

LENGTH: 24-1/2 inches (61 cm)

WING SPAN: 47 inches (1.2 m)

LIFE SPAN: 12 to 20 years

SPECIAL DESIGN FEATURE: The raven is a sophisticated flyer and can do numerous aerial stunts.

DID YOU KNOW? The raven is considered to be one of the most highly intelligent birds in the world.

Common Snipe

How many of us have gone snipe hunting as children at dusk? With flashlight in hand, we looked through bushes, behind rocks and trees, only to be fooled. We finally realized we had been set up and there is no such thing as a snipe. But there is such a creature! It is a small brown bird with a long, pointed beak. It is most active in the evening and early morning.

This shy bird is a close relative of the woodcock, inhabiting marshes and wetlands. It flies in a zigzag pattern, holding its beak in a downward position.

The eyes of the snipe are black and set well back in the head. The plumage is camouflaged and is barred tan to a deep reddish-brown and is mottled, with a cream-colored belly. The general appearance of the common snipe is similar to other waders such as the sandpiper. However, the thin legs of the snipe are shorter.

The dark brown bill is flexible and soft skinned, and the tip is almost prehensile as it is used to probe inside the soft earth searching for food. The bill is so flexible that the snipe can eat some food while the beak is buried in the soil. The diet of the snipe consists of snails, insects, and a wide selection of worms.

The snipe is also famous for its courtship. This small bird flies high then dives, holding its wings half-closed, beating them slowly while fanning its tail. The air passing through produces the well-known drumming sound of the snipe.

All snipes nest on the ground with the exception of the New Zealand snipe, which uses the burrows of other birds. In the hollow grass-lined nest, a clutch of three to four olive-brown eggs is laid. The female incubates the eggs for 19 to 20 days. The young leave the nest almost immediately. They are fed by both parents and can fly in about two weeks.

Snipes can be found in North America, New Zealand, Australia, New Guinea, Asia, Africa, and Europe.

Common Snipe

CHARADRIIFORMES • SCOLOPACIDAE
GALLINAGO GALLINAGO

LENGTH: 10-1/2 inches (27 cm)
WEIGHT: 11-1/4 ounces (320 g)
LIFE SPAN: 20 years
SPECIAL DESIGN FEATURE: The long bill of the snipe is particularly flexible at the tip, allowing it to probe and eat while the beak is buried in soil.
DID YOU KNOW? Because of children's games, many think the snipe to be a myth. The snipe is a very unique and real bird.

Emperor Penguin

The emperor penguin is one of the largest, and hardiest of the seabirds. It makes its home in the harsh climate of Antarctica on the barren ice packs and along the coastlines. Enduring sub-zero temperatures and hurricane force winds, the penguin can survive in these extreme conditions because of its thick plumage. Two dozen short and stiff feathers per square inch with a downy base trap a layer of warm, insulating air. Having their body low to the ground helps as well by keeping the cold air out.

The upper part of the penguin's body has black feathers and the lower body is white with a yellowish tinge. It almost looks as if it were wearing a tuxedo. There is a very distinctive broad yellow marking on its neck.

The emperor penguin feeds on squid and fish that it pursues underneath the water, catching them in its long razor-edged bill. The inside of the mouth and tongue are covered with backward pointing knobs which help prevent the fish from slipping out. The penguin does swallow a considerable amount of seawater but the excess salt is excreted through large salt glands just above the eyes. It can dive after food as deep as 870 feet (265.2 m) and hold its breath for 18 to 20 minutes. Its heavy body is one factor which enables the emperor penguin to dive deep.

In April and May, the penguins gather for mating at the rookeries (nesting areas) which are located inland on solid ice. In August, each female lays one large egg, which is carried on the feet and covered with a fold of skin. It is passed between the female and male until the female heads off to feed in the open water a few days after the egg is laid.

The male incubates the egg for 40 to 50 days, shielding it from the sub-zero weather with a fold of skin. Penguins huddle together to keep warm. The warmest place is in the middle of the group. They keep moving in and out of the huddle so that every bird gets a chance to get warm in the center of the huddle. The female returns a few days before the egg hatches to finish the incubation and the male goes to sea to feed. Upon hatching, she stays with the chick for approximately 40 days. By mid-January, the chick has shed its coat of down and has its adult plumage. The chick is on its own now as they all leave the rookery.

The penguins have few predators because of the barrenness and fierce cold of Antarctica, but occasionally adult penguins are taken by leopard seals or killer whales. Young penguins are stalked by the giant petrel.

Emperor Penguin

SPHENISCIFORMES • SPHENISCIDAE
APTENODYTES FORSTERI

WEIGHT: 66 pounds (30 kg)

LENGTH: 45 inches (115 cm)

LIFE SPAN: 20 years

SPECIAL DESIGN FEATURE: The emperor penguin survives the coldest weather in the world, having a thick layer of feathers that are short and stiff with a downy base.

DID YOU KNOW? The emperor penguin can dive up to 870 feet (265.2 m) and stay underwater for 18 minutes.

Great Blue Heron

Standing as an elegant sculpture, the great blue heron remains motionless in the shallow water. When a fish comes within striking distance, the great blue heron will either spear or grab its meal and swallow it whole. Some herons have tried to swallow fish so large that the bird choked to death. These large birds can be seen fishing in lakes, rivers, marshes, streams, backyard pools, bays, ocean shores, tidal flats, and sandbars.

The great blue heron ranges from southeast Alaska and southern Canada as far as southern Mexico, the Galapagos Islands, and the West Indies. In Florida, there is a white color phase of the great blue heron.

Its long black legs allow it to wade in the water. The heron has the patience of Job as it waits on its prey. Three-fourths of the heron's diet is fish but it will also take snakes, salamanders, frogs, insects, ground squirrels, young muskrats, shrimp, crayfish, and crabs. The long, sharp, pointed yellow beak is a weapon and a wounded bird can be dangerous. One struck a pine oar with such force that the beak protruded two inches (5.2 cm) on the other side.

When the great blue heron flies it has a slow wing beat, and travels at about 30 mph (48 km/h). Unlike geese and cranes, the heron doesn't stick its neck out when flying, but carries its head against its body, hiding its long neck while its legs stick out behind. The wing span can be up to 7 feet (2.1 m) but most average 5 to 6 feet (1.5 to 1.8 m). When standing, they can be 4 feet tall (1.2 m).

The great blue heron is entirely gray-blue in color except for some white around the head and part of the neck. Some may have cinnamon-colored necks and legs, although the legs are normally black. It has a black stripe above the eye, which is yellow, the same as the bill.

The bird is usually silent; however, when startled, the heron makes a croaking sound, and while in flight, it honks.

The nest of the blue heron is usually 20 to 100 feet (6.1 to 30.5 m) above the ground on rocks and cliffs and is made up of small sticks. There may be only a few or up to hundreds of nests built in one area used by a group of herons. Both sexes incubate the three to seven blue-green eggs. The eggs hatch in 25 to 29 days and the chicks leave the nest in 62 to 90 days.

Great Blue Heron

CICORIIFORMES • ARDEIDAE • ARDEA HERODIAS

HEIGHT: 4 feet (1.22 m)

LENGTH: 42–52 inches (107–132 cm)

LIFE SPAN: 11 to 21 years

SPECIAL DESIGN FEATURE: The sharp, long, pointed bill of the heron can either grab or spear its prey.

DID YOU KNOW? One wounded heron struck a pine oar with such force that its beak protruded two inches (5.2 cm) on the other side.

Great Cormorant

The great cormorant can be found worldwide on the coasts of the North Atlantic, southeastern and northern Europe, East and South Africa, South and East Asia, parts of Central Asia, Japan, Australia, and New Zealand.

The great cormorant has a very sleek shape, dark in color with a long neck and a long, serrated beak with a hooked tip. The chin and sides of the face are white. The strong webbed feet give it power underwater.

Because its feathers are not waterproof, the cormorant can often be seen perched on a rock, tree, or boat with its wings outstretched as it dries its feathers. However, some believe that they are not drying feathers, but catching thermal heat to raise their body temperature.

Its feeding grounds are shallow, inshore waterways where it can dive to catch its prey. When it reaches its prey, it snaps its bill shut, gripping the fish with its serrated beak as it brings it to the surface to swallow it. Fish are the main food, but cormorants also catch crabs, eels, and frogs. They dive and swim underwater using their tail as a rudder and strong thigh muscles and webbed feet for propulsion. The cormorant can stay submerged for up to 60 seconds and can dive 30 feet (9.1 m).

The great cormorant nests in both coastal and inland areas in trees, on the ground, and on cliffs. The nest is a mound made of sticks and dried seaweed about three feet across. Both parents incubate three to four eggs for about 28 or 29 days. They feed the chicks for about two months and the young will return to the nest site to feed for another six weeks.

Fishermen do not like to see their rival, the cormorant. However, in parts of Asia, people use the cormorant to catch fish for them. Placing a ring around the cormorant's neck to prevent it from swallowing the fish, they put it on a long rope enabling it to hunt underwater for the fish.

Great Cormorant

PELECANIFORMES • PHALACROCORACIDAE PHALACROCORAX CARBO

WEIGHT: 4 to 8 pounds (1.81–3.63kg)

LENGTH: 36 inches (92 cm)

LIFE SPAN: 20 years

SPECIAL DESIGN FEATURE: A sleek shape, a long serrated bill and powerful webbed feet equip the great cormorant for catching its prey.

DID YOU KNOW? In parts of Asia, people use cormorants to catch fish. They tie the birds to boats with long leads and allow them to hunt underwater. A ring around the bird's throat prevents it from swallowing the fish.

Greater Flamingo

The greater flamingo is found in the Americas from the Bahamas to Tierra del Fuego, including the Galapagos Islands and from southern Europe to South Africa across to India.

This strange-looking bird is known for its long neck, long legs, and pink color. Its plumage is tinged with pink except for the black flight feathers. Having very tough skin on its legs, it can withstand extremely alkaline soda and salt lagoons which would take the skin from a person's legs in seconds. The flamingo's knees are really the ankles and when it sits, the ankles bend backwards.

Flamingos live in great flocks around lakes and lagoons where food can readily be found. Their diet consists of protozoa, algae, crustaceans, mollusks, and insects. The pink color of the plumage actually comes from chemicals called carotenoids, which are contained in the algae eaten.

When feeding, it wades through the water with neck lowered and head upside down, swinging from side to side. The tongue acts like a pump pulling in the water and food as a row of bony plates sieves the food from the water. The flamingo then filters the water out. The combination of backward-pointing spines on their palate and a unique tongue guides the particles down the throat.

Flamingos breed in great colonies. The male and female together build the nest, which is located in the center of a huge mud flat where predators can't reach it. The nest is a mound of mud 12 to 20 inches (4.73 to 7.88 cm) in diameter with a depression on top for the egg. It has to be tall enough to keep the egg away from any spray that might blow up.

A single egg is laid and is incubated by both parents for approximately 30 days. The parents feed regurgitated liquid called "crop-milk" to the chick until it is able to feed itself. The bill of the hatchling is not curved when it is born but will develop its characteristic shape later. The chicks can swim in 10 days and it takes about 10 weeks for them to grow their feathers.

The main enemy of the flamingo is the fish eagle that picks off young flamingos. Other enemies are hyenas, cheetahs, and jackals.

In ancient Rome, flamingo tongues were a delicacy. Flamingos and their eggs were also eaten until recently.

The flamingo has to build up speed for a long take-off, but once in the air they fly very well with slow, lazy wingbeats.

Greater Flamingo

PHOENICOPTERIFORMES • PHOENICOPTERIDAE PHOENICOPTERUS RUBER

WEIGHT: 6 to 7 pounds (2.72–3.18 g)
LENGTH: 50–78 inches (127–200 cm)
WING SPAN: 70 inches (187 cm)
LIFE SPAN: 27 to 50 years
SPECIAL DESIGN FEATURE: The bill of the flamingo is lined with a filter of bony plates to trap planktonic food and keep large particles of soil and other debris out.
DID YOU KNOW? The knees of the flamingo are really the ankles and bend backwards when the bird sits down.

Great Horned Owl

The great horned owl lives in most areas of North and South America including forests, deserts, and even in cities. Sometimes it is possible to locate owls by listening for their very distinctive hooting call.

The feathers of the horned owl are dark brown with black markings on the upper part of the body and lighter brown with black horizontal bars on the lower part. Owls have large forward-pointing eyes, which are circled by large zones known as facial disks, two areas usually white in color and half-moon shaped. This particular species has its ears covered by tufts of feathers that look like horns and give the great horned owl its name. The bowl shape of the facial disks helps funnel sound to the ears, giving the owl excellent hearing.

Like most birds, it has four toes, but while most birds have three front toes and one in back, the owl can rotate its outer third toe to the back, giving it two in front and two in back. This helps the mighty raptor capture and grip its prey more easily. The curved, pointed beak of the owl can rip its prey to shreds, but it likes to swallow its prey whole if possible.

Sight is especially acute in this bird of prey. Their large eyes with a bright yellow iris are designed with a highly developed lens and cornea and a special opaque membrane on their eyelid. This third eyelid is called the nictitating membrane and it is used to protect the sensitive retina from the bright light of the daytime. Like other birds, the eyes are fixed in their sockets so that the owl cannot move them up and down or to the sides. Therefore, it must turn its whole head to move the eyes. They have a frontal vision field of 70 percent. However, they can rotate their heads very rapidly about 270 degrees, which increases their vision field tremendously.

As a nocturnal hunter, the owl needs outstanding vision, but also relies on its acute hearing to locate and catch food. The ear structure is very well designed with the right and left ears often differently shaped. A moveable skin fold along the front edge of the ears reflects sound waves from behind them.

The diet of the great horned owl is mice, rabbits, frogs, squirrels, muskrats, snakes, opossums, and even skunks. The owl can stealthily attack its prey because of serrations on the front edge of the first primary feathers allowing it to fly silently. They can attack at speeds of up to 40 mph (64 km/hr).

The great horned owl does not usually build a nest but uses tree hollows, burrows, or the nests of other birds such as eagles or hawks. The female lays 1 to 5 eggs and incubates them for 35 days. The young can fly at 9 to 10 weeks.

Great Horned Owl

STRIGIFORMES • STRIGIDAE • BUBO VIRGINIANUS

WEIGHT: 8-3/4 pounds (4 kg)

LENGTH: 17–21 inches (43–53 cm)

WING SPAN: 35–60 inches (92–154 cm)

LIFE SPAN: 29 years

SPECIAL DESIGN FEATURE: The great horned owl's eyes are located toward the front of its head but the head can be rotated 270 degrees, greatly increasing its vision range.

DID YOU KNOW? The great horned owl is the largest and most powerful of all North American owls.

Hoatzin

The hoatzin bird lives in the dense rain forests along streams and rivers in South America.

The hoatzin is a very colorful bird with a blue head, a tuft of feathers standing up on the head, and an orange iris in the eye.

The upper parts of the hoatzin's body are brown with whitish streaks on the back. The feathers on the neck and breast are fawn-colored with the underparts being reddish-brown. The hoatzin is about the size of a chicken.

The main source of food for the hoatzin is leaves and fruits of aquatic plants. Arum plants are a large part of their diet. Because leaves are hard to digest, God designed the hoatzin with an extra stomach, called a "crop," in its throat. This crop has special enzymes which break down the leaves before they enter the regular stomach.

The nesting spot for the hoatzin is located on a limb just above the water surface of a stream. The female lays two to five eggs, which hatch after 28 days. The hatchlings are naked at birth but are able to move around. They can leave the nest after three days. They will follow other members of the family around in the trees begging for food. The baby chicks have two claws on their feet and two wing claws, which make it possible for them to scramble over the branches in the trees. When danger approaches, the little chick will climb away from the danger or, if it must, it can dive into the water and swim to safety. When the danger is past, the hoatzin climbs back up into the tree.

The young hoatzin learns to fly when it is about six weeks old. To learn to fly well can take up to four months, and when they have mastered flying, their wing claws drop off.

Usually, a family flock will help in raising the young by building the nest, sitting on the eggs, and feeding the young. The family flock consists of the parents and older offspring, which may linger in the flock for 4 to 5 years.

Hoatzin

GALLIFORMES • OPISTHOCOMIDAE OPISTHOCOMUS HOAZIN

WEIGHT: 28.5 ounces (800 g)

LENGTH: 24 inches (60 cm)

SPECIAL DESIGN FEATURE: The young hoatzin has two claws on its wings to help it climb around in the trees but these atrophy when they learn to fly.

DID YOU KNOW? Although it is not an aquatic bird, a young hoatzin can swim if it falls into the water.

Laughing Kookaburra

One of the most easily recognized birds in Australia is the kookaburra, a large kingfisher which lives in parks, woodlands, and forests in eastern Australia. The kookaburra has been introduced to western Australia and is also found in Tasmania.

The plumage of the kookaburra is dark on the back down to the rusty-colored tail. The wings are dark also with white markings on them. The kookaburra is white or light gray elsewhere except for the black slash across the eyes. The heavy beak is dark on top, yellow-brown on bottom, and is approximately 3 to 4 inches (8 to 10 cm) long.

If you are in the Australian bush and hear loud laughter, it is probably a kookaburra claiming territory. The sounds of this noisy bird were used in the old Tarzan movies even though it lives far from the African jungle.

Kookaburras like to perch on a branch or wire searching for prey. Peculiarly, they are known as kingfishers, but their diet consists not of fish, but of invertebrates — lizards, snakes, frogs, small mammals, and other birds. Catching its prey on the ground, the kookaburra will carry it into a tree or onto a large rock and then bash it on the branch or rock to kill it. Sometimes, they drop their prey to the ground, smashing it and killing it.

The nest of the kookaburra is made in hollow trees or in a termite mound. If it uses a termite mound, it digs a burrow into the mound and leaves it for a week. During this time, the termites seal their tunnels making it more comfortable for the birds. One to four white eggs are laid and incubated by both parents and a "helper" for about 25 days. These "helpers" are young birds around four years of age that have not mated. The helpers aid in 30 percent of the incubation and up to 60 percent of food gathering for the chicks. Young birds are born naked but in a week or two start growing feathers which are protected inside sheaths until the hatchling is ready to leave the nest in about 30 days. Parents continue to feed the young birds for another 40 days. While inside the nest, the young also feed on the remainder of insects, pellets, and small flies that have been consuming eggshell debris. Young kookaburras autograph their nest entrance by backing up to the nest opening and depositing their waste. This is called "signposting."

There are about 85 species of known kingfishers worldwide. How many would God have had to bring to Noah and his family for the ark? Only one male and one female.

Laughing Kookaburra

CORACIIFORMES • ALCEDINIDAE
DACELO GIGAS

WEIGHT: 14 ounces (380 g)

LENGTH: 17 inches (22 cm)

LIFE SPAN: 12 years, although some in captivity may live 20 years

SPECIAL DESIGN FEATURE: The long, strong bill of the kookaburra allows it to capture a variety of small prey.

Did you know? The cry of the kookaburra sounds like loud human laughter.

Osprey

The osprey of North America, known as the fish hawk, is successful 90 percent of the time at making its catch. It soars 25 to 100 feet (7.62 to 30.5 m) above fresh or salt water using its keen eyesight to spot a fish. When it sees the target, it will dive into the water, creating a huge splash. The osprey disappears under the water surface for a second, then becomes airborne again with a fish hooked in its sharp talons. It shakes the water from its feathers in midair and repositions the fish so its head is pointed forward, reducing flight drag. It then flies to a perch to enjoy its meal. Not all catches are so dramatic. Sometimes it is fortunate enough to catch a fish with only the feet having to enter the water.

The osprey mainly eats fish but has been known to occasionally take small birds, rodents, snakes, frogs, and sometimes ducks. If a bald eagle is close enough and sees an osprey catch a fish, it will dive at the osprey causing the osprey to drop the fish in flight and many times the eagle will catch the fish before it hits the water.

The osprey is about the size of a small eagle with a 5-foot (1.5 m) wingspan. The undersides of the feet of an osprey are designed to hold slippery fish. They are covered with spiny scales to create a grip. Two long toes point forward and two point backward aided by sharp talons which assure successful strikes.

The head of the osprey has a short crest, which is an off-white color, and there is a dark mask running through the eye joining the dark brown plumage on the back. The eyes are yellow-orange and the beak is black. The belly is whitish.

Ospreys live on every continent except Antarctica, nesting in colonies or singly in dead or partially dead trees close to the water. The osprey is almost cosmopolitan and sometimes builds nests on utility poles, chimneys, and buildings, using sticks, bones, seaweed, corn stalks, and beach junk. The nest is added to each year and can end up weighing one-half ton (454 kg), lasting for decades.

The osprey lays two to four eggs that are a white-to-pinkish color with dark spots. In North America, the female does the incubating but in other parts of the world the eggs may be incubated by both sexes. The male will feed the female during incubation, which lasts 35 to 38 days. The young chicks will make their first flight in 7 or 8 weeks.

Osprey

FALCONIFORMES • PANDIONIDAE
PANDION HALIAETUS

LENGTH: 22 inches (55 cm)

WING SPAN: 54–72 inches (1.27–1.83 m)

LIFE SPAN: 21 years

SPECIAL DESIGN FEATURE: The undersides of an osprey's feet are covered with spiny scales and its long toes have sharply curved talons to hold onto slippery fish.

DID YOU KNOW? The osprey is successful in 90 percent of its attempts to catch fish, a remarkable average among predators.

Ostrich

The ostrich inhabits parts of the Soviet Union, China, India, and southern and eastern Africa. It is the largest living bird in the world and is easily recognized by its shagged black feathers growing along its back and white flight and tail feathers. The ostrich cannot fly but runs at speeds of 44 mph (70 km/h) — the fastest running bird in the world. (The fastest running-flying bird is the roadrunner.)

The ostrich feeds on grasses, leaves, shoots, and some insects. Unique among birds, the ostrich can store its urine in the cloaca and release it separately from its solids.

The ostrich is well-designed for its environment. An ostrich has only two toes on each of its strong feet, which can produce a very powerful kick. The eyes on its small head are sharp and quick to spot predators such as lions or cheetahs. Long lashes protect their eyes from dust storms in the open scrub and savannahs. Like a periscope, the long neck raises and lowers helping the ostrich scan its habitat. When running, the long featherless legs of the ostrich make 10-foot (3 m) strides at a time. The flightless wings help maintain balance in a fast run.

The ostrich is a curious bird and will often pick at objects better left alone. For instance, ostriches have been known to swallow necklaces, clocks, pencils, rope, etc.

Man has successfully domesticated the ostrich and ostrich farms are not uncommon. They are farmed for their delicious meat, feathers, leather, and eggs from which ornaments are made. Domesticated ostriches can be dangerous and this big bird must be handled with care.

The mating season varies. The male digs a shallow hole in which the female lays her 8 to 10 eggs — the largest-sized egg of any living bird. (It takes 20 chicken eggs to equal the volume of one ostrich egg.) Other females may lay eggs in the same nest. The dominant female chases the other hens away and she and her mate share in the work of incubation. Within 39 or 40 days, the chicks will begin to hatch. Hatching may take up to 2 days. When the chicks are a few months old, they are on their own and will form large groups. Males will mature in three to four years and females in about two to four years.

An ostrich does not bury its head in the sand, but will sometimes lie flat on the ground with its neck and head straight out in front of it, making the head difficult to see, thus causing some to think that the head is buried in the sand.

Ostrich

STRUTHIONIFORMES • STRUTHIONIDAE STRUTHIO CAMELUS

HEIGHT: Male: 8 feet (2.5 m)
Female: 6 feet (1.8 m)

WEIGHT: Male: 330 pounds (150 kg)
Female: 200 pounds (90.7 kg)

LIFE SPAN: 40 years

SPECIAL DESIGN FEATURE: The ostrich has long, powerful legs making it the fastest running bird in the world.

DID YOU KNOW? The ostrich is the largest bird in the world.

Pileated Woodpecker

The pileated woodpecker is the largest woodpecker in North America. This crow-sized woodpecker can be found in woodland areas from southern Canada and across the northern and central United States. There are 200 species of woodpeckers spread over the forests of the world except in Madagascar, Australia, and other oceanic islands.

Pileated woodpeckers prefer to live solitary lives in the deep woods of mature forests, but have had to adapt to living in forests with younger growth trees.

They are black in color with a red crest on both the male and female. The male has a red streak running from the corner of its mouth back to the crest. The beak is black and the chin white.

Woodpeckers are excellent tree climbers, having two backward facing toes, sharp claws, and stiff tail feathers, which are used as a prop while climbing. Starting at the bottom of a tree, a woodpecker goes in a spiral motion around the tree searching for insects. You can certainly hear the tapping noise as its beak strikes the tree rapidly and repeatedly.

The diet of the pileated woodpecker includes ants, flies, mosquitoes, moths, grubs, seeds, walnuts, and acorns. Using its pointed bill to chisel into the wood of trees, it hammers away as it searches for food. Its brain is cushioned inside the strong skull so that it is not smashed as the woodpecker drills into a tree. Because one little twist of the neck could be fatal, strong muscles hold the neck straight when hammering. God's design of every aspect of the woodpecker is magnificent and perfect. The woodpecker certainly could not have survived any evolutionary plans that man could come up with.

Woodpecker tongue

When the hole is drilled, the woodpecker uses its extremely long tongue (6 inches–2.34 cm) to reach inside to get the insects. At the end of the tongue are bristles like a brush to spear the insects. When not in use, this long tongue is wrapped along the back of the skull and inserted in the right nostril.

The nest of the pileated woodpecker is usually a triangular-shaped hole bored high in a tree. Two to eight eggs are laid and incubated by both parents for approximately 18 days. The young will leave the nest when they are 22–26 days old.

Pileated Woodpecker

PICIFORMES • PICIDAE • DRYOCOPUS PILEATUS

WEIGHT: 10–16 ounces (285.7–457.1 g)

LENGTH: 16 inches (42 cm)

WING SPAN: 27–30 inches (69.2–76.9 cm)

LIFE SPAN: 9 to 13 years

SPECIAL DESIGN FEATURE: The skull, brain, and neck muscles of the woodpecker are designed to take the force of impact as the woodpecker hammers into a tree trying to find a meal.

DID YOU KNOW? The woodpecker can eat up to 2,000 ants a day.

Ptarmigan

There are three species of ptarmigan that live in the northern areas of Scandinavia, Siberia, Alaska, arctic Canada, Greenland, and Iceland, with an isolated population in Europe and Asia.

The ptarmigan lives among rocks with little vegetation at an altitude of 2,000 feet (609.6 m) or more in severe habitat.

This unique bird has three different plumages. In the spring and summer, the upper parts are spotted gray or brown, the wings and underside are white. In the winter, the ptarmigan is completely white except for black on its tail and the male has black eye patches. The whiteness of the plumage in winter serves as more than camouflage as it also reduces heat loss from the body. In the early spring or fall, the feathers are a mixture of brown and white as they change from one color to the other. It also has feathers on its legs and toes allowing it to walk on top of the snow. There is a red wattle over each eye.

In the winter, the ptarmigan can burrow under the snow as a shelter to spend the night. In the summer, it likes to sunbathe and roll in the dust.

It feeds mainly in the early morning or early evening on a diet consisting of seeds, bulbs, shoots, leaves, berries, and insects.

Ptarmigans fly up and down with ease over hollows and hills. They walk with a rolling gait and when alarmed, they crouch low to the ground. Their plumage, whatever the season, serves as excellent camouflage blending into the colors of the ground. They fly only when danger is close.

In the spring, the female will make a small clearing, which serves as a nest among short grass or low plants. She lays 5 to 9 eggs at intervals of 1 to 2 days. When her clutch is complete, only the female will incubate while the male keeps close watch nearby. The chicks hatch after 24 to 26 days and are tended by the female while guarded by the male. They are able to fly in about 10 days. The family stays together until autumn when several birds come together to form a large flock.

Some of the enemies of the ptarmigan include birds of prey, fox, and lynx.

Ptarmigan

GALLIFORMES • TETRAONIDAE
LAGOPUS MUTUS

WEIGHT: 15–20 ounces (425–600 g)

LENGTH: 14 inches (35 cm)

LIFE SPAN: 4–10 years

SPECIAL DESIGN FEATURE: The feathers of the ptarmigan change color with the seasons.

DID YOU KNOW? The legs and toes of the ptarmigan are covered with feathers enabling this bird to walk on snow without sinking.

Rainbow Lorikeet

The rainbow lorikeet is a medium-sized parrot that lives in northern and eastern Australia. The plumage of this bird is very bright and colorful. It has a red bill, blue head, bright green upperparts, red-gold breastband, and a blue belly.

The beak of the lorikeet is not raspy like other parrots but it does have a long, hair-tipped tongue that laps up nectar and pollen from blossoming flowers. It actually crushes the blossoms with its beak and laps up the juices with it tongue. It can be a pest when it descends upon an orchard. The orchard floor can be littered with crushed and fallen blossoms. It also feeds on fruit and sap.

These beautiful birds can be found in light woodlands and scrub areas but also can adapt quite well to large towns where they even visit garden feeders. They are not afraid of people and seem quite tame. At the Currumbin Bird Sanctuary in Queensland, rainbows come by the scores to be fed by hand. Each visitor gets to hold a tray of honey water that the lorikeets love. At about 4:30 in the afternoon, the lorikeets descend on the trays to eat. They walk all over the visitors' heads and arms to get to the tray. You can actually watch their tongues lap up the sweetened water.

Lorikeets usually move in flocks and are swift in flight, having a high pitched screech that is unmistakable. Roosting in camps or flocks, they screech and chatter until ready to go to sleep.

Lorikeets pair for life and the nests of the lorikeets can be found in the hole of a tree or an empty cavity high above the ground. The female usually lays two eggs, which are incubated by her for about 3 to 4 weeks. Both parents feed the young hatchlings which leave the nest approximately 9 or 10 weeks after hatching.

The enemies of the lorikeet are birds of prey such as the goshawk.

Rainbow Lorikeet

PSITTACIFORMES • PSITTACIDAE
TRICHOGLOSSUS HAEMATODUS

LENGTH: 6–16 inches (15–40 cm)

LIFE SPAN: 20–40 years

SPECIAL DESIGN FEATURE: God designed this parrot to show off almost all the colors of the rainbow.

DID YOU KNOW? The tongue of the lorikeet is like a brush, mopping up nectar and pollen from fruit.

adrunner

ne has enjoyed the antics of the
and the coyote in comics and
life, the roadrunner looks a lot
eally is the world's fastest running-
ostrich is the fastest non-flying bird.)

is a bird of prey and sometimes is
e mongoose of the bird family for
h snakes, even venomous ones. This
s placed the roadrunner in exagger-
ends. The roadrunner's diet consists
ainly on the ground such as insects,
s, small rodents, birds, and snakes.

the roadrunner is brown streaked
ings on the upper part and a dirty
h. The legs and beak are blue. They
st on their head. Roadrunners have
d the eye, which is broader at the
e two toes pointing forward and two
ard. Its long tail, which is as long as
dy, is used as a rudder to help
er the bird as it runs.

ird can fly but is rather awkward
ort wings. It was designed to run,
ave been recorded as high as
h). Fifteen mph (24 km/h) is generally
vith the average being 10 mph
amazing sprinter darts and scampers
sand taking 12 steps per second
n shrubs and cactus.

makes its home in southwestern
and central Mexico in deserts which
s ground-dwelling predator often
n the desert heat and becomes active
. Although the days are hot, the
n drop very low at night. To

compensate for the low temperatures, the roadrunner allows its temperature to drop slightly each night and goes into a state of torpor, which is similar to hibernation. In the morning as the sun rises, there is a special patch of dark-colored skin between the wings of the roadrunner that absorbs heat quickly, warming the skin and blood vessels. This helps the bird reach its normal temperature for the day.

The nest of the roadrunner is made of twigs in a shallow basket-like bowl found in brush or cactus, often as high as 17 feet (5 m) off the ground. The female lays two to nine white eggs and incubates them for about 18 days. At about 8 days they can walk and perch. In three weeks, the young are able to run and find their own food.

The roadrunner has few enemies but relies on its speed to escape them.

Roadrunner

**CUCULIFORMES • CUCULIDAE
GEOCOCCYX CALIFORNIANUS**

WEIGHT: 18 ounces (500 g)

LENGTH: 23 inches (58 cm)

LIFE SPAN: 14 years

SPECIAL DESIGN FEATURE: The long tail of the roadrunner is used for balance and as a rudder for maneuvering as it darts after its prey.

DID YOU KNOW? The roadrunner has been recorded at speeds of up to 26 mph (42 km/h) — approximately 12 steps per second, making its legs a blur.

Ruby-throated Hummingbird

In the sun, the feathers of the hummingbird flash a metallic green and the throat of the male sparkles a fiery red color. The wings beat so rapidly that they appear as a blur creating that humming sound. High speed photos revealed that the hummingbird beats its wings 55 times per second when hovering, 61 per second when backing up, 75 per second when flying straightway, and 200 per second during courtship. No other bird can out-perform the flight maneuverability of the hummingbird.

One-third of this bird's total weight is made up of breast muscles. The energy needed is phenomenal — it eats twice its body weight everyday. Operating at the same energy level as this tiny bird, our hearts would beat 1,260 times a minute and our body temperature would be 385 degrees centigrade. We would explode!

The hummingbird has a needle-like bill that penetrates deep into flowers to extract nectar. A long, trough-like tongue holds the nectar; this tongue can dart into the flower and be licked 13 times per second. This little bird is attracted to red flowers but also feeds on honeysuckle, petunias, lilacs, and other flowers, aiding in pollination. It is also fond of some insects and spiders. It will sometimes get into battles with bees over feeding rights.

The ruby-throated hummingbird migrates more than 1,850 miles (2,977 km) from Nova Scotia, Canada, to Central America, flying between 55 to 60 mph (89 to 97 km/h). Before migrating, the hummingbird will put on a fat layer equal to half of its body weight for traveling fuel.

During courtship, the male makes a display for its mate by flying back and forth in an arch. The female builds a small nest out of lichen and leafy materials, usually between 5 and 20 feet (1.5 to 6.1m) off the ground. During the night, hummingbirds enter into torpor, a sort of temporary hibernation. A nesting female, however, stays awake and keeps her eggs warm. The female incubates two white bean-sized eggs. In 16 days, the chicks hatch and are fed nectar and small insects. In three to four weeks, they leave the nest. Females are thought to return to the same nest every year. During incubation, the male may look for another mate.

Hummingbirds are spunky and attack birds much larger than themselves such as eagles and crows. Their enemies are large spiders, praying mantises, frogs, and dragonflies, just to name a few.

Ruby-throated Hummingbird

APODIFORMES • TROCHILIDAE
ARCHILOCHUS COLUBRIS

WEIGHT: 1/10 ounce (3.11 g)

LENGTH: 4 inches (10.16 cm)

LIFE SPAN: 5 years

SPECIAL DESIGN FEATURE: The hummingbird can hover and fly forward or backward by beating its wings an incredible 90 times or more per second.

DID YOU KNOW? You would need to eat 1,300 hamburgers a day washed down with 63.4 quarts (60 liters) of water to equal the energy needed each day by the hummingbird.

Secretary Bird

The secretary bird can be found in the southern two-thirds of Africa in the open grasslands, plains, and savannahs. It searches for food where the vegetation is not too dense for it to run. It is a very fast runner.

In appearance, the secretary bird looks like a crane, having very long legs that are covered with feathers to the knees. Its tail has two long feathers sticking out, and its feathers are gray with black on the wings and legs. On each side of the face is a patch of bare, red skin and on the back of the head is a crest of long black-tipped feathers. These long, flowing feathers hang down, resembling quill pens that clerks carried in their wigs in the 18th century, and that is what gives this bird its name.

The secretary bird is a bird of prey and it spends much of its time on the ground hunting for food. It does not migrate unless the food supply is short. Unlike other birds of prey, the secretary bird does not have grasping toes that are used to seize prey. Its short, blunt toes are armed with curved talons.

The diet includes a wide variety of animals, locusts, insects, small mammals, young birds, snakes, tortoises, and lizards. The method of hunting is to walk through the grass, stomping occasionally to flush out prey. Small animals are caught in its bill but larger animals and snakes are killed by trampling them.

The nest of the secretary bird is built in the top of the acacia tree and is made up of sticks lined with grass. It can be 8 feet (2.4 m) across. Two or three eggs are laid and incubated by the female for about six weeks. Both parents feed the young for about seven months. The chicks will stay with their parents for some time after they learn how to fend for themselves.

The secretary bird is a good flyer but prefers to walk. It needs a long runway for takeoff.

Secretary Bird

FALCONIFORMES • SAGITTARIIDAE
SAGITTARIUS SERPENTARIUS

HEIGHT: 4 feet (1.2 m)
WING SPAN: 7 feet (2.1 m)
SPECIAL DESIGN FEATURE: The secretary bird has long legs that are feathered down to their knees. It looks like they are wearing pants.
DID YOU KNOW? The secretary bird can kill a snake up to 4 feet (1.2 m) long.

Sulfur-crested Cockatoo

This spectacular-looking parrot can be found in Australia and New Guinea. There are 18 species of cockatoo found in the Australia/Asia region. White plumage consisting of feathers that are hard and glossy with powder-down mixed through them, and a black beak characterize the physical appearance of the bird, which receives its name from the tuft of yellow feathers on its head. The cockatoo has two toes that point forward and two that point backward. It is Australia's best-known bird and is transported the world over as a pet that can be taught to mimic humans.

The cockatoo lives in most types of open wooded country along rivers and waterways. In the southern part of Australia, cockatoos live in large flocks except during the breeding season. In northern Australia, they are in pairs or small groups throughout the year. Each group has a favorite roosting place, preferring a dead, isolated tree.

The only difference between the male and female of the species is eye color. The female has reddish-brown to deep red eyes and the male has brown eyes. Like other parrots, the upper bill of the cockatoo is attached to the skull by a flexible joint, coming to a sharp point and fitting over the lower bill. It has powerful tongue and jaw muscles.

Cockatoos spend their mornings searching the ground for seeds, nuts, berries, fruits, flowers, corn, and small insects. There is usually one bird standing guard which warns of approaching danger with a loud screech. By noon, the birds fly into the trees to seek the shade and keep busy by stripping the bark and leaves off of the trees they are in. In the cool of the afternoon, they again drop to the ground to feed before heading to roost at dusk.

The nest of the cockatoo is found in a hole in a tree or the high part of a riverside cliff. The female lays two eggs on a pile of wood dust at the bottom of the hole. Incubation is mainly the female's duty and lasts 30 days. Both parents care for the young.

This bird is protected in nearly all of the Australian states, however, farmers can get a permit to shoot them when they destroy crops.

Sulfur-crested Cockatoo

PSITTACIFORMES • CACATUIDAE
CACATUA GALERITA

LENGTH: 20 inches (50 cm)

LIFE SPAN: usually 50 years

SPECIAL DESIGN FEATURE: This is one of the best-known birds of Australia. The cockatoo makes a wonderful pet and they can be taught to mimic human language.

DID YOU KNOW? The oldest-recorded age of any bird was the 80 years of a sulfur-crested cockatoo that died at the London Zoo in 1982.

Toco Toucan

Thirty-three species constitute the toucan family, with the toco toucan possessing the largest bill. Its territory ranges from the rain forests of eastern Brazil to forested areas along the rivers of northern Argentina and in palm groves with large trees.

This large bird does not fly well but its very strong legs allow it to remain in the treetops, hopping from perch to perch. Its natural enemies are not known, but the toucan can be tamed as a pet. These particular birds bathe high in the treetops using pools of rainwater found in the hollows of trees.

Toucans have a black body with a white patch under the throat and face and a patch of white just above the tail. The most distinctive part of this bird is its large bill, which is orange, black, and hollow inside, making it very light. Although lightweight, this bill is very strong, having a network of support rods on the inside. The toucan uses its bill and six-inch (2.37 cm) tongue to pick up food.

The notches along both edges of the tongue make it like a brush at the end, enabling it to gather food easily. The toucan feeds on fruit, berries, seeds, insects, and spiders, and sometimes eats small lizards, snakes, and eggs. This large-billed bird will hold food in its bill and throw back its head, tossing the food down its throat. If the food is too large, it will tear off pieces with its bill.

The toucan nests in a tree that has a hole formed by decaying wood. It does not line its nest but regurgitates seeds to form a bed. The female lays 2 to 4 eggs and both parents take turns incubating them for about 16 days. The young are born blind and naked. Both parents feed the hatchlings during the several weeks of development. A layer of feathers can take about 30 days to grow.

Toco Toucan

PICIFORMES • RAMPHASTIDAE
RAMPHASTOS TOCO

WEIGHT: 1 pound (457.1 g)

LENGTH: 2 feet (60 cm)

LENGTH OF BILL: 8 inches (20 cm)

LIFE SPAN: 30–50 years

SPECIAL DESIGN FEATURE: This large bird cannot fly well but has toes that give it a good grip to hop from limb to limb in the trees.

DID YOU KNOW? The toco toucan is the largest member of the toucan family and one-third of its length is its bill.

Turkey Vulture

The turkey vulture, commonly called buzzard, is a blackish-colored bird with a reddish, featherless head. Not known for physical beauty, vultures soar gracefully and elegantly in thermals, hardly ever flapping their wings. In flight, they can be distinguished from other large birds by the position of the wings. Eagles and hawks soar with wings stretched horizontally but vultures soar with wings slightly lifted in a wide "V" shape.

Most people think of the vulture as a revolting bird because of its eating of dead flesh. The people who classified this amazing bird, however, were aware of its usefulness and named this genus of vultures Cathartes, meaning "purifier." Vultures rid our countryside and garbage dumps of unwanted waste and are truly our volunteer purifiers.

Bacteria which can carry disease can pass unharmed through the digestive system of most animals but the potent digestive juices of the vulture kill all bacteria entering into these scavengers. It has been stated that we may never know how many serious epidemics have been stopped because of the vulture.

Vultures can sometimes be seen sitting on fence posts holding their wings outstretched. This possibly serves two purposes. One purpose is to cool the bird and the other is to allow the long rays of the sun to help destroy bacteria on the feathers.

There has been a debate for centuries as to how the vulture actually finds its food, either by sight or smell. Audubon did an experiment and hid a carcass from sight with canvas. The vultures weren't attracted to it. When he put a picture of a dissected sheep on the canvas, the vultures came. A man named Mr. Bachman covered a decaying carcass with canvas and then put meat on it. The vultures ate the exposed meat but left the putrid meat, which was only inches from their nostrils. However, a number of times vultures have gathered over leaks in gas pipes, indicating they were attracted by the smell.

Vultures must allow meat to partially decay or tenderize before consumption because their beaks are weak. Vultures sometimes eat live prey, taking mice, nestlings, and even eggs.

Most vultures migrate in the winter. Buzzards nest at ground level in hollow trees or stumps. The nestlings are snow white.

The turkey vulture has few natural enemies, but man has killed a number of vultures with his automobile.

Turkey Vulture

FALCONIFORMES • CATHARTIDAE CATHARTES OURA

WEIGHT: 2-3/4 pounds (1.3 kg)

LENGTH: 29 inches (74.4 cm)

WING SPAN: 4–6 feet (1.2–1.8 m)

LIFE SPAN: Average 20 years; known to have lived in a zoo for 50 years.

SPECIAL DESIGN FEATURE: The turkey vulture's appetite for carrion helps purify our countryside.

DID YOU KNOW? Turkey vultures find their food mainly by keen eyesight.

Wild Turkey

Both sexes of the wild turkey are large, but the male is larger than the female. Mature males are called toms, younger males are called jakes, and the females are called hens. The tom turkey has long, coarse bristles, called a beard, hanging from its breast. When sportsmen hunt wild turkey, usually only males may be taken. One of the ways the male is recognized is by its long beard.

The plumage of the wild turkey is dark on the body with iridescent green and bronze highlights as light is reflected off the feathers. Females are duller in color. The legs are a bright reddish-pink and the males have sharp spears on the inside of their legs like most game birds.

During the spring mating season, toms will show off for potential mates. Fanning their tail feathers wide, they puff up their body plumage, dragging their wings on the ground and making a drumming sound as they strut. Toms are also called gobblers and live up to their name. They gobble in the spring and any loud noise can set them off — a car door slamming, airplanes flying over, or even another bird.

The naked head has very few small hairs and feathers. The male has a "snod" or fleshly carbuncle at the base of its beak, which can lengthen or shorten according to the mood of the bird. The color of the head can also change rapidly to white, purple, blue, red, or anything in between, depending on the bird's mood. Turkeys have extremely sharp eyesight which pick up the slightest movement, and are therefore very challenging to hunt.

This shy bird lives in open and mixed woodlands moving in small flocks, feeding during the daytime and roosting high in the trees at night. It is a strong flyer but will only fly short distances; upon landing, it will quickly disappear into the forest.

Turkeys eat insects, plants, seeds, nuts, and berries — quite a variety of food. In the wild, its enemies include the owl, fox, raccoon, opossum, and coyote.

As the nesting season approaches, each day the female lays one brown egg in a depression in the ground, continuing until a total of 9 to 14 eggs complete the clutch. She incubates the eggs for approximately 28 days, and after hatching the chicks will leave the nest, staying with the mother. The young are able to fly to roost in about two weeks, but are very vulnerable and half will be killed off by fall. Remarkably, the greatest single threat to the young is rain because they have no protection against getting soaked.

Wild Turkey

GALLIFORMES • PHASIANIDAE
MELEAGRIS GALLOPAUO

WEIGHT: 24 pounds (11 kg)

LENGTH: 40–50 inches (100–125 cm)

LIFE SPAN: 8–12 years

SPECIAL DESIGN FEATURE: The turkey's shy nature and sharp eyesight enable it to survive by being so cautious that any slight movement or sound will cause it to flee.

DID YOU KNOW? Benjamin Franklin wanted the wild turkey to be the national bird of the United States because of its courting behavior.

Wood Duck

One of the most beautiful ducks in the world is the wood duck. The magnificent plumage of the male includes a back covered with metallic, iridescent blues and greens, a reddish-brown breast with white spots, and a beautiful, dark green-blue crest outlined in white on the head. The eye of the male is bright red and the beak is brightly colored as well with black, whitish-cream, red, and yellow. The female has a gray back with blue on her wings, and brown eyes. The belly of the wood duck is white and its webbed feet are yellow, marked with a few dark stripes. To see the detailed beauty of this bird demands praise to the almighty artist who created it.

Freshwater birds, wood ducks inhabit wooded areas, living by the ponds, lakes, rivers, and streams of the United States and parts of Canada. Some will stay in their northern range for the winter season, but others will migrate a relatively short distance in small flocks.

In flight, the wood duck can be identified by the rapid beating of its wings and the whistling sounds it makes. They are adroit flyers and can dart between tree branches even at dusk.

Wood ducks feed on a varied diet including floating plants, seeds, and bulbs, along with wild celery, wild rice, docks, and grasses. Insects such as dragonflies and beetles, snails, amphibians, minnows, and even acorns that have fallen to the ground, are also ingested by this bird.

Wood ducks prefer to nest in a hollow tree crevice, possibly the abandoned nest of a squirrel or woodpecker. The nest can be between 5 and 50 feet (1.83 and 15.24 m) above the ground, usually near water, but if it has to, the bird will move inland to find a place to nest. Squeezing inside a very small hole to nest is no problem for the hen, which lays a clutch of 6 to 15 eggs, hatching in approximately 29 days. The male stays near the nesting site during the incubation period, but after hatching, it is the mother that calls the ducklings to her on the ground. The hatchlings must leap from the nest, which may be very high. Both parents will then hurriedly lead the young to the safety of the water.

At one time, the wood duck was the most abundant duck in the United States. However, early in the 20th century, fears of its soon extinction mounted as its numbers depleted. Through years of proper wildlife management, the wood duck has made a remarkable recovery. Raccoons, snakes, minks, otters, and in the south, alligators, are all natural threats to the wood duck.

Wood Duck

WEIGHT: 1-1/2 pounds (685.7 g)
LENGTH: 18-1/2 inches (47 cm)
LIFE SPAN: 4-1/2 to 8 years
SPECIAL DESIGN FEATURE: Baby wood ducks leap from their nest to the ground (which can be 50 feet (15.24 m) above the ground) right after they are born.
DID YOU KNOW? The wood duck is one of the most colorful ducks in the world.

Intelligent Design

ARCHAEOPTERYX – 100% BIRD

The famous fossil of archaeopteryx, found in Berlin in 1877, has often been hailed as the desperately needed missing link that evolutionists have long hoped for. Many have said this fossil bird clearly shows reptilian features such as teeth, claws on the wing, and a skeleton that looks similar to a Coelurosaurian dinosaur, *Compsognathus*. However, looking closely at archaeopteryx has shattered the hopes of the kinship between this bird and the dinosaur. Some differences worth noting include the upper jaw and the brain. In vertebrates, including reptiles, only the lower jaw or mandible moves. In birds, the upper jaw, or maxilla, moves as well, as was the case in archaeopteryx. Archaeopteryx had a brain like that of flying birds with a visual cortex and a large cerebellum. The wishbone (furcula) was robust which is a design of a flying bird.

Archaeopteryx had teeth but so did other birds in the fossil record. There is a species of hummingbird today in South America, known as the tooth-billed hummingbird, that has teeth. The three claws on the wings of archaeopteryx have also been used to justify the dinosaur-to-bird link but to no avail. There are birds alive today that have claws on their wings. The young hoatzin and the ostrich have claws on their wings.

The similarities found in the skeletons of most vertebrates do not show proof of evolution. God, in His wisdom, used a basic plan that works. No one would believe that a John Deere tractor evolved into a Mercedes. Yet they both have many of the same features.

The hind toe (hallux) of archaeopteryx is that of a perching bird and not like the dewclaw (first digit) of a dinosaur.

Archaeopteryx had 100 percent feathers and no in-between scale-to-feather features. There has never been a scale-to-feather intermediary organ found in the fossil record. Most ornithologists at the International Archaeopteryx Conference in Eichstatt, Germany, in 1984 accepted and believed archaeopteryx was a fully formed bird.

The long tail of archaeopteryx had 20 vertebrates and each shows trace fossils of feather imprints. The feathers on the tail show no sign of being broken or having frayed tips, which would be suspected on a ground dweller, which helps verify that archaeopteryx was a tree dweller.

"In spite of some paleontologists' desperate pleas for us to accept through faith the dinosaurian origin of birds, and therefore the ground-up origin of avian flight, the details of the origin of birds remain elusive after more than a hundred and fifty years." (Alan Feduccia, *The Origin and Evolution of Birds* [New Haven, CT: Yale University Press, 1999])

FEATHERS

Most evolutionists believe scales evolved into feathers. The theory goes like this: Through mutation, reptilian scales grew longer and longer, fraying over the course of time, and feathers evolved by random chance. Those who believe this today are without excuse. Photos taken under the scanning electron microscope tell the story.

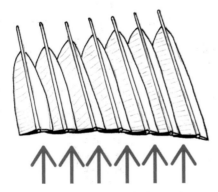

Made up of keratin, feathers are light and strong with countless complex features that demand that the hand of God created them. The primary feathers on the wing are absolutely astonishing. When one of the primary feathers molts, the other wing loses the same feather at the same time! They also grow back in matched pairs so the bird will not be off-balance, allowing it to fly symmetrically. The primary feathers are attached to muscles, which give the bird the ability to shape and angle its feathers by rotating them in flight. The tail on a peacock is a great example of how muscles attached to the feathers can be used as they fan their tail.

AIR PRESSURE ON DOWNSTROKE

The barbs close like slats on a blind on the downward stroke. Lift and propulsion are accomplished by this stroke. Very little air flows through.

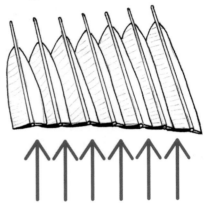

The Creator designed the barbs of the second and primary feathers to allow the air to flow through reducing drag on the upstroke.

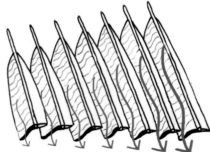

Feathers are waterproofed by applying oil from an oil gland at the base of the tail. Birds use their beaks to routinely oil their feathers as they groom and "zip" them back together. (Everyone has picked up a feather and zipped the separated barbs back together.) The feather is actually like velcro. Under the electron microscope, it shows the tiny hooklets that fit into grooves, repairing the feather in a velcro-like manner.

There are different types of feathers. On the breast of the bird there are feathers called "afterfeathers." These are down feathers or insulating feathers and are used to keep the bird or its brood warm. Anyone owning a down sleeping bag knows the insulating capabilities of these feathers.

Another type of feather can be seen when a bird is plucked as small hairs over the bird's body. These small hairs are actually tiny feathers (called filoplumes) and are now believed to be receptors monitoring the position of the surface feathers of the bird's body. These receptor feathers signal to the other feathers how to position for takeoff and gliding, and the degree of ratio needed.

The number of feathers on a bird depends on the kind of bird and the time of year. A house sparrow has approximately 3,546 feathers, while a whistling swan has approximately 25,216 feathers. Most birds have between 1,500 to 3,000 contour feathers (feathers making up the surface plumage besides the wing and tail feathers).

COLOR

Birds have three kinds of color. The flamingo's pink color is a good example of the color in a bird's feathers which comes from excrement. This pink color is produced by waste products from the food it eats being absorbed into the feathers. Zoos are very careful to feed the birds their native foods for this reason. The pigment melanin produces the soft yellow, brown, black, and red colors in birds. The third kind of color is iridescent and it is due to an interference layer on the feathers. The iridescent color is the result of the barbules of the feather.
(See illustration of the feather on page 72.) Light rays strike the feathers from different angles,

scattering and refracting brilliant colors of green, red, and purple.

LUNGS

The trachea (windpipe) has two parts. One in front of the lungs and one at the back of the lungs, growing into air sacs in the bones, making the respiratory system of birds the most efficient of all vertebrates. These balloon-like air sacs are extensions of the lungs and branch to different parts of the bird's body, even extending to the toes. Between 6 and 14 air sacs provide comfort in most birds by operating as indirect air exchangers and regulating the body temperature of the bird, which has no sweat glands. The air sacs also help to give the water birds

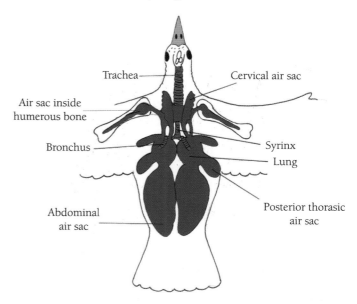

RESPIRATORY SYSTEM

buoyancy, make birds lighter for flight, and cushion the blow as a pelican hits the water in a dive for food. Some birds, such as the frigate bird, use the air sacs to inflate their necks as part of their courtship behavior.

CIRCULATORY SYSTEM

Not only the respiratory system but also the circulatory system of a bird is more efficient than that of mammals. Since these warm-blooded animals need so much energy when flying, God has designed them with a complete double circulatory system that utilizes energy in a most capable manner. The heart of a bird is about 40 percent larger than mammals of the same size. It beats approximately 35 times less rapidly yet pumps the same volume of blood. As a rule, the smaller species have comparatively bigger hearts.

BONES

God designed the bones of most birds to be hollow, filled with air spaces instead of marrow. This design makes the bones light while the honeycombs of trusses or struts make them very strong. The four-pound frigate bird possesses a large seven-foot wing span, yet its skeleton weighs only four ounces (113 grams). The bird's feathers weigh more!

CROSS SECTION OF BONE OF A BIRD SHOWING AIR SPACES

BILL (BEAK)

The bill or beak is an extension of the bony jaws. The upper half of the bill, called the maxilla, is quite flexible and the bird is able to move it slightly, increasing its gape. The upper jaw in parrots is especially flexible because of a well-designed hinge between the bill and the skull.

Depending on the beak, the bird can use it to tear, cut, or crush its food. It can also be used as a chisel to dig out insects like the woodpecker uses its beak. In most birds, the tip of the beak wears down with use, especially on ground-feeding birds. Fortunately, the bill grows and renews itself continuously toward the tip.

THE BRAIN

The entire brain is located in a small space toward the back of the bird's head. It is quite a bit larger (ten or more times) than that of a reptile and very different. The large optic lobes allow for keen eyesight but they are located at the sides of the brain instead of in the roof of the midbrain as in reptiles and mammals. The olfactory lobes are relatively small giving the bird a poor sense of smell.

The cerebrum of the brain is relatively smooth and lacks the folds of a mammal's brain. The cerebellum, which handles the precise control of the bird's movements, is very well designed. The cortex or outer layer of gray matter is not large and does not make direct contact with the spinal medulla. The part of the brain that controls the reflex activity of the skeletal muscles, the "rhombencephalon," is very well designed to maintain muscular tone and body posture.

EYES

Birds have very acute eyesight, equal to humans, but birds can pick up details and movement faster. Usually the largest part of a bird's head, the eyes often weigh more than their brain. The eye of a hawk or owl is comparable in size to a man's, but the ostrich has the largest eye of all birds. More sensory cells are in the eye of a bird than any other animal, especially in the area of the fovea, a small depression in the retina at the point of the sharpest vision. The fovea helps magnify the image in view about 30 percent in some birds.

Birds have what is called a third eyelid or nictitating membrane to clean and moisten the cornea. The eyes are fixed into their sockets so they must turn their heads to look. Owls can rotate their heads about three-fourths of a full circle.

All birds have monocular (one-eyed) vision, the ability to see independently with each eye, and binocular (two-eyed) vision, the ability to see straight ahead. The area that a bird sees is very different among the different species of birds.

The shape of the eyeball is determined by the size of the sclerotic ring, a series of thin, bony plates surrounding the cornea. The eyeballs of most diurnal (active in daylight) birds have a flattened, disc-like shape, like swans. The more tubular-shaped eyes belong to nocturnal birds such as owls and those with the keenest long-distance sight such as eagles.

Cones and rods in the retina of the bird are receptors, which form the image that the bird sees. Cones operate in the daylight, enabling the bird to receive sharp images. The rods function at night or in low-light conditions and are especially abundant in the eyes of owls. Color vision of birds is not very different from what humans see.

EARS

Hearing ranks next to sight in importance to a bird's survival. Birds are highly social and they depend on hearing other birds to detect predators and danger.

Ear openings for most birds are on the side of the head, hidden by feathers. For most birds, there is no fleshy outer cartilage to catch sound waves, but owls have a moveable skin fold along the front edge of the ears to reflect sound from behind. Feathers covering the ears are called auriculars. Having no barbules, they do not interfere with the hearing.

The cochlea of a bird has a response speed ten times faster than that of humans. Owls especially have very acute hearing. The ears of birds consist of a sensory receiving apparatus in the internal ear as well as an external ear and a middle ear. These function to collect and amplify vibrations from the air.

Sound enters the small ear opening (external auditory canal) which ends at the eardrum (tympanic membrane). Sound then enters the middle ear, an air-filled cavity extending from the eardrum to the outer bony wall of the internal or inner ear. The middle ear connects with the back part of the bird's mouth (pharynx). It houses a single earbone called the columella which has one end attached to the eardrum, while the other end is in contact with an oval opening in the wall of the inner ear. From here, sound travels to the cochlea. The cochlea is the auditory part of the inner ear, which transforms sound waves to nerve impulses conducted to the brain by the cochlear nerve. Did all of this happen by chance? To God be the glory.

The hearing of birds is so sensitive that they were kept during WWI to give warnings of approaching airplanes that were too far away to be heard or seen by humans. Some domesticated birds are also used as watchdogs because of their acute hearing ability.

"Behold the fowls of the air: for they sow not, neither do they reap, nor gather into barns; yet your heavenly Father feedeth them. Are ye not much better than they?" (Matt. 6:26).

THE END

Bird Skeleton

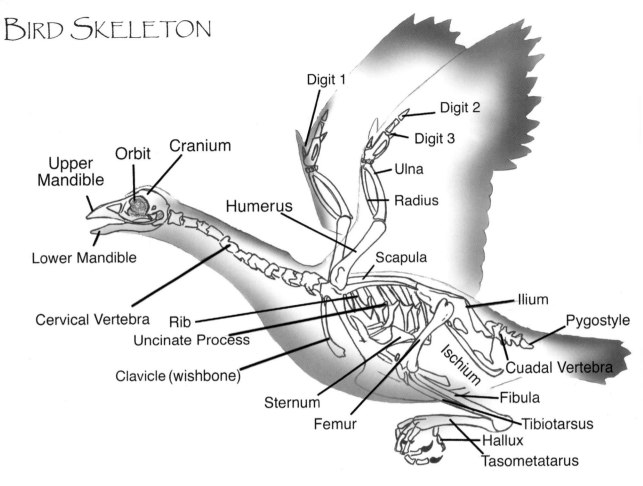

Digit 1

Digit 2

Digit 3

Ulna

Radius

Upper Mandible

Orbit

Cranium

Humerus

Scapula

Lower Mandible

Cervical Vertebra

Rib

Uncinate Process

Clavicle (wishbone)

Sternum

Femur

Ilium

Pygostyle

Cuadal Vertebra

Ischium

Fibula

Tibiotarsus

Hallux

Tasometatarus

Types of Bird Feet

SWIMMING

ANCHORING

RUNNING

PERCHING

SNOW SHOES

GRASPING

PARTS OF A BIRD

BEAK

EYE

EAR

Wing

Coverts

Throat

Primary feather

Breast

Secondary feather

Belly

Leg

Tail feathers

Foot

BIRD SKELETON

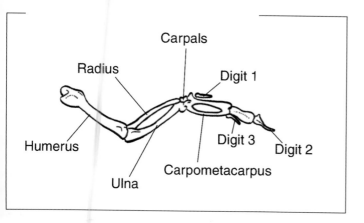

Carpals

Radius

Digit 1

Humerus

Digit 3

Digit 2

Ulna

Carpometacarpus

Types of Bird Beaks and Their Purposes

INSECTS

CRUSHING SEEDS

TEARING

SPEARING

SKIMMING

NETTING FISH

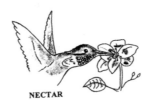
NECTAR

DRILLING

FORAGING

SIPHONING

PROBING

Bibliography

Angell, Tony. *Owls*. WA: University of Washington Press, 1974.

Attenborough, David. *The Life of Birds*. Princeton, NJ: Princeton University Press, 1998.

Bologna, Gianfranco. *Simon & Schuster's Guide To Birds of the World*. New York: Simon & Schuster, 1978.

Bright, Michael, editor. *The Wildlife Year*. London: The Reader's Digest Association, Inc. 1993.

Brooks, Bruce. *On the Wing: The Life of Birds from Feather to Flight*. New York: Charles Scribner's Sons, 1989.

Bull, John and John Farrand Jr., editors. *National Audubon Field Guide to North American Birds — Eastern Region*. New York: Alfred A. Knopf, 1994.

Burn, Barbara. *North American Birds, The National Audubon Society Collection Nature Series*. New York: Gramercy Books, 1991.

Burton, Dr. Maurice, and Robert Burton, editors. *Funk & Wagnalls Wildlife Encyclopedia* Vol. 1,2,3. New York: B.P.C. Publishing Ltd, 1970.

Cassidy, James, editor. *Book of North American Birds*. New York: Reader's Digest Association, Inc., 1990.

Chapman, Geoff. "Weird and Wonderful — The Penguin." *Creation Ex Nihilo,* 11(4), Sept.–Nov. 1989, p. 28.

Chinery, Michael. *The Kingfisher Illustrated Encyclopedia of Animals*. New York: Kingfisher Books, Grisewood & Dempsey Inc., 1992.

Dock, George. *Audubon's Birds of America*. New York: Harry N. Abrams, Inc., 1979.

Feduccia, Alan. *The Origin and Evolution of Birds*. New Haven, CT: Yale University Press, 1999.

Forbush, Edward Howe and John Bichard May. *A Natural History of American Birds*. New York: Bramhall House, 1955.

Hall, Francis W. *Birds of Florida*. St. Petersburg, FL: Great Outdoors Publishing Company, 1994.

Hennigan, Tom. "A Wonderfully Bizarre Bird." *Creation Ex Nihilo*, 19(4), Sept.–Nov 1997, p. 54–55.

Hussong, Clara. *Birds*. Racine, WI: Western Publishing Company, Inc. 1973.

Jakob-Hoff, Richard, and Beryl Marchant. *Birds of Western Plains Zoo*. Dubbo, NSW, Australia: Western Plains Zoo, 1987.

Juhasz, David. "The Incredible Woodpecker." *Creation Ex Nihilo*, 18(1), Dec. 1995–Feb. 1996, p. 10–13.

Mackay, John, editor. "Did You Know? The Amazing Arctic Tern." *Creation Ex Nihilo*, 9(2) March 1987, p. 20.

Mathewson, Robert. *The How and Why Wonder Book of Birds*. New York: Wonder Books, 1960.

Menton, David. "Bird Evolution Flies Out the Window." *Creation Ex Nihilo*, 16(4), Sept.–Nov. 1994, p. 16–19.

Book of Birds. Philadelphia, PA: Courage Books, 1990.

Parish, Steve. *Amazing Facts About Australian Birds*. Queensland, Australia: Steve Parish Publishing Pty Ltd, 1997.

Parish, Steve. *First Field Guide to Australian Birds*. Queensland, Australia: Steve Parish Publishing Pty Ltd, 1997.

Peterson, Roger Tory and the editors of *Life*. *The Birds*. New York: Time Incorporated, 1963.

Pough, Richard H. *Audubon Land Bird Guide — Birds of Eastern and Central North America from South Texas to Central Greenland*. New York: Doubleday & Company, Inc., 1949.

Rue II, Leonard Lee. "Game Birds of North America." *Outdoor Life*. New York: Harper & Row, 1973.

Saunders, David. A *Grosset All-Color Guide — Sea Birds*. New York: Grosset & Dunlap, 1973.

Scott, Shirley, editor. *Field Guide to the Birds of North America*. Washington, DC: The National Geographic Society, 1991.

Scott, Sir Peter, editor. *The World Atlas of Birds*. New York: Random House, 1974.

Shortt, Terence Michael. *Wild Birds of the Americas*. Boston, MA: Houghton Mifflin Co., 1977.

Sparks, John and Tony Soper. *Owls — Their Natural and Unnatural History*. Newton Abbot, Great Britain: David and Charles Ltd., 1972.

Stokes, Donald and Lillian. *Stokes Field Guide To Birds — Eastern Region*. New York: Little, Brown and Company, 1996.

Terres, John K. *The Audubon Society Encyclopedia of North American Birds*. New York: Alfred A. Knopf, 1982.

Welty, Joel Carl. *The Life of Birds*. Philadelphia, PA: W. B. Saunders Co., 1975.

Wexo, John Bonnett. *Zoobooks — Eagles*. San Diego, CA: Wildlife Education Ltd, 1983.

Wieland, Carl, editor. "Strong, But Special — Toucans." *Creation Ex Nihilo*, 20(4) Sept–Nov 1998, p. 34–35.

Wildlife Explorer. Stanford, CT: International Masters Publishers, AB, 1998.

Williams, Winston. *Florida's Fabulous Waterbirds*. Tampa, FL: World Publications, 1983.

Zim, Herbert S. and Ira N. Gabrielson. *A Guide to the Most Familiar American Birds*. New York: Golden Press, 1956.